How to Sell Annuities.
Annuity Sales Techniques, Tips and Strategies.

By Michael Bonilla

About the Author.

We're all salespeople. Some less direct than others, but we all have to sell. Whether you are interviewing for a job or trying to convince your kid to clean their room. Ever since I can remember I've always had an interest in the power of persuasion. How do some people tend to always get what they want. Some people use authority and some people use cleverness. What I've found is that your ability to understand people generally will support or conversely under-mind your ability to convince and lead people.

As a rule of thumb with my books. I'd like them all to be easy to read. Easy to digest. Full actual application and proven systems. If you can read my book in a single sitting, then I consider that to be successful.

"Annuities are not usually bought they are sold."
-Unknown

Contents

1. Introduction
2. Fundamental Sales Tips
    a. Sales Rules
3. What an Annuity?
    a. How does an Annuity work?
    b. Understand Two Strategies.
4. Which types of Clients are Annuities suited for?
5. Marketing Annuities
    a. Where to Market.
    b. Meeting with the Decision Maker.
    c. Find A Mentor.
6. Areas of Concerns for Retirees
    a. 3 Most Common Problems in Retirement
7. 3 Common Sources of Income for Retirees
8. How Annuities can fill the gap for a retiree.

"Quality is not an act, it is a habit."

- Aristotle

Chapter 1: Introduction

If there is a single take away from this book, remember this, selling insurance is a process. It's a process that is a both an art and a science. That being said, every sale no matter how unique the client the overall process remains more or less the same. People tend to give you the same objections and tend to walk along similar lines of thinking.

Whether you are a seasoned insurance veteran or a new entry, this book might be just what you are looking for. I like to think that there are golden nuggets of wisdom in this book. If you find something useful, use it.

Selling an Annuity requires a somewhat different approach when you compare it to other insurance products. An annuity is really an investment vehicle that is an insurance product. Unlike, a life policy that is a life insurance product that can be an investment vehicle.

Purchasing life insurance or in this case an annuity isn't like purchasing a bar of soap at the grocery store. There should be a good amount of consideration and thought that comes along with the purchase.

Applying for insurance is a lot like applying for a job. Do you always get every job that you apply for? Not usually.

It's also unique in that it is something you have to qualify for. As a professional take the time to learn your product and your craft. It's easy to get an insurance license but when we talk about retirement planning we are talking about people's money.

Have you ever heard people say that life insurance and annuities are an emotional sale? The key difference from what separates a great life agent and a price driven life agent is the ability to tether a life insurance policy or in this case annuities with personal experiences of the insured. How do you make this policy meaningful to the prospect?

This business has always been a relationship business and for the foreseeable future that should remain relatively true. Of course, this is easier said than done. So, in this book we will cover how to evoke those emotions, understanding clients and developing value based sales approaches.

That being said don't force ideas on people just give them something to think about and they will arrive at the same conclusion.

As you read this book I want you to begin to think about selling in a different light. Selling is a lot like Texas Hold'em. Poker is classified as a limited information game. Which means each hand you are granted limited information to make a decision. Each hand has what are called implied odds. Just like in selling people are not always open books. You have to take time to 'read' them and understand what they care about. You have X amount of information and you have to make a decision. How you process that info will determine for the most part the outcome of a sale. This is why understanding each client on an individual level is so important. Understanding and addressing their concerns and questions and overall understanding what they need and what they want.

My favorite poker player is Daniel Negreanu. The reason why is he is a talker. By talking he is able to read people and get information that isn't on the board.

As an Agent our job is to help clients make educated and informed decisions. So, how do we do that? We have to see what cards everyone is playing with. Figure out why the person is looking to buy, find out if there are gaps in the current plan, find out if the person is a think or feel person and find out what the person cares about.

"You must understand fear so you can manipulate it. Fear is like fire. You can make it work for you; it can warm you in the winter, cook your food when you're hungry, give you light when you're in the dark and produce energy. Let it go out of control and it can hurt you, even kill you…fear is a friend of exceptional people." **– Cus D'Amato**

Chapter 2: Fundamental Sales Tips

Rule Number 1: Don't Complicate Something.

Rule number one of selling insurance is to keep it simple. We are selling insurance not building a space ship. Explain the concepts in digestible terms that consumers can understand and stray away from using too much insurance jargon.

Once I sat thru a long sales consultation with a rep for a large life insurance company. The rep had a well thought out, but thoroughly confusing Indexed Presentation. After about 45 minutes of this rep carrying on I started wondering if she actually was going to talk about how the product actually worked or anything that might be relevant to product features

Rule Number 2: Always be agreeable.

Selling is as much an art as it is a science. There is no formula for agreeableness. Just know that the more confrontational the worse your odds are for closing.

Rule Number 3: Understand the Person.

Don't make snap judgements about what someone can afford. Dig.

There are two types of people that sit in front of you. There are think type of people and feel type of people. What I mean is that people respond to questions in different ways. Some people say, "I think..." and some people say, "I feel..."

The reason why you need to grasp this concept, is the fact that during a sale we have these invisible boundaries. Emotional or feel people require stories and think people require figures and facts. Not everyone is the same. But, there is a limit for feel people and there is a limit for think people that we have to monitor in the sales process.

Rule Number 4: The Person Needs to Understand you.

Ask yourself does the prospect have enough information to know, like and trust me? If not then you need to build that trust through conversation. Through asking questions.

Rule Number 5: Reciprocity

If an insurance sale is a search for the truth we need to follow the rule of reciprocity. The rule of reciprocity makes the insurance buying process a collaborative effort not a confrontational one.

Remember you make no money until the person signs up with you, so you are educating them for free. This is the key to reciprocity. You ask questions to evoke emotions during the process and client has questions that you answer to provide certainty.

The reason why we focused so much on processes in this book is because each sale is more or less always going to be the same. It has an opening and a closing and in between you talk about stuff.

Rule Number 6: Stick to a process.

Every person is different, but every sale is exactly the same. In that, people give you the same responses, the same objections and will follow a path. When you start selling insurance it's important to remember that you have a start, you build rapport, you ask questions that are open ended, you find a problem if one exists, and you build a solution/close.

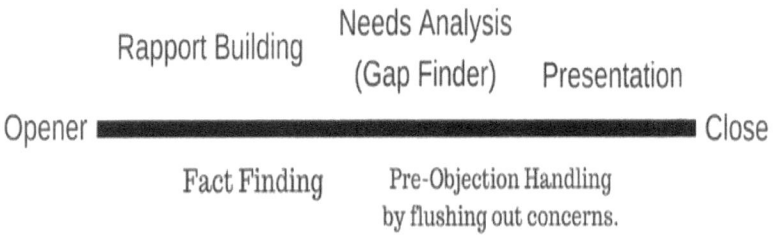

Rule Number 7: Know When To Close and Know When to Fold.

Some prospects believe it or not just enjoy talking to sales people and have no intention of buying. Being a salesperson you must think that is somewhat crazy, I did. But, it's true.

During your presentation it's important to know when people are giving off buying signals and asking buying questions.

Think of a sale like a Turkey in the oven. First you have to marinate the turkey. Then you preheat the oven. After your prep work is complete and the oven is at the right temperature you put the Turkey in the oven. Some turkeys require more prep work because some are FROZEN and some are fresh. You cook the turkey and check the temperature along the way. But, you have to keep marinating the turkey as it cooks. If the internal temperature is correct after X amount of hours you pull it out and it's moist. If you leave it in too long it dries out or maybe even burns or becomes ruined.

I'll make an effort to dispense with the food analogies for the rest of the book. Think of it this way. Think of it like an index. The 'Closability' index. Some people are easier to close than others and some require a tremendous amount of effort. But, either way the prospect will ask buying questions.

Well, what's a buying question? For instance, "How much does this cost?" If you are not interested in a product you do not ask how much it will cost. Simple.

Rule Number 8: Ask Open Ended Questions

If you are new to sales or new to insurance. Your best friend is the ability to ask open ended questions and leading questions.

Would you mind if we talked about open ended questions? This is a directive question asking for permission to ask a question.

How do you feel about annuity sales? What do you think about annuity sales? Whatever the answer always remember to ask follow up questions. You have two ears and one mouth so as a ratio ask too questions before you start to babble on about insurance.

Rule number 9: Set Expectations

You need to set boundaries. What should a client come to expect of you? What do you expect of a client?

A lot of Agents (including myself) tell a client that they meet with each client once per year to make sure the insurance is current or on target. There is nothing customized about that statement for a client. Instead why not just ask. How often would you like to meet each year to discuss your insurance? Most of my clients find once a year to meet their needs but some prefer a call once a quarter to check in.

Rule Number 10: Don't lose control of the conversation.

Probably the most common challenge for newer agents is not maintaining focus. A prospect is going to focus on price if you let them and it can derail the conversation.

Price is merely the cost of value. It's your job to educate and present the value. Remember you are the expert and what you focus on will direct the conversation. Don't avoid talking about price, but at the same time don't rush or lead with price. See Diagram Below.

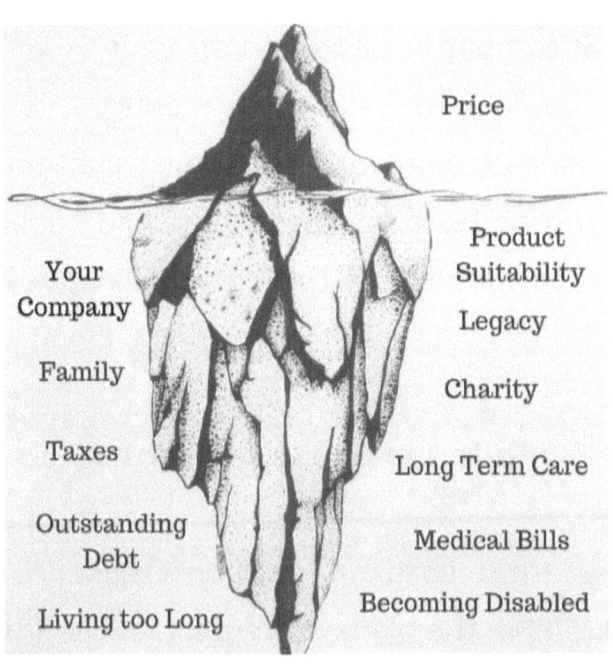

Rule Number 11: Don't always try to reinvent the wheel.

My father was a carpenter and used to say the nail that sticks out tends to get hammered. Craft your approach as you learn your trade. If your trade is selling insurance, then read, apply and learn.

It's important as you craft your style/approach to make adjustments. Somethings might work and some might not. But, start by learning from others and adopting an approach and then putting your unique spin on it.

Rule 12: Speak in Furturo

Learn to speak in the future tense. As your Agent... fill in the blank statement. While I was going to college I paid my way by being a Personal Trainer. I learned very quickly to speak in the assumptive future tense. As your blank... here's how I can be of service to you. "Well, I haven't said I would sign up with you yet." This is the response I want to hear from a client, a soft objection or they might ask buying questions and be able to be closed on the spot. I'm planting seeds not seeds of doubt. But, planting a picture in their head to so some thinking. Picturing in their head hwo working with me is going to look like and benefit them.

"Experience alone does not create knowledge."
– Kurt Lewin

Chapter 3: What is an Annuity?

In this book we are going to cover a lot of ground. We are going to talk about the ins and outs of annuity sales. We are going to cover how Annuities work, which clients annuities are suited for, strategies to sell annuities and much more. The first question we have to ask is how does an Annuity work.

How does an Annuity work?

Generally speaking an annuity is a tax deferred insurance product where you give the life insurance company X amount of dollars starting around $10,000.

The life insurance company will invest your money and pay you a certain percentage of interest in return. There are surrender charges, possible riders and death benefit components for some annuities.

Note from Author: This book is sales focused more than product focused. If you have specific annuity product questions make sure to ask your TPA or insurance company.

Types of Annuities

For the purposes of this book we are going to talk about two kinds of annuities Indexed and Immediate Annuities with Guaranteed Payments for life.

Understanding Two Strategies

The best way to learn how to sell Annuities is by learning two simple strategies and building from there. Once you have learned those two strategies learn two products that can fit client's needs within those strategies

Strategy 1: Indexed or Variable Annuity

The easiest strategy revolves around addressing key areas of concern (discussed later) and leveraging money sitting in savings accounts. Savings that are just sitting around earning less than 1% interest. For this strategy just learn and understand Indexed Annuities and Variable Annuities. This strategy is a standalone annuity that is replacing money the client just plans on sitting around in a savings account for an extended time horizon. It's simple and it's merely a 'all-in' style approach for 5 to 10 years.

Usually Annuities to be effective require large lump sums to fund. Keeping that in mind the first strategy is selling the safety and security of an indexed annuity with a 5 to 10 year time horizon.

Strategy 2: Immediate Annuity to Fund a Life/LTC.

The second strategy is somewhat more complex. The second strategy involved selling an immediate annuity and leveraging the income to purchase a permanent life insurance policy to match the amount of money put into the annuity and then add a disability/LTC rider or purchase a standalone LTC policy. Basically, you can leverage the income into purchasing two other life products and still have money left over for additional income.

Because your own strength is unequal to the task, do not assume that it is beyond the powers of man; but if anything is within the powers and province of man, believe that it is within your own compass also. **Marcus Aurelius**

Chapter 4: Which Clients are suited for Annuities?

This question is somewhat open ended. Because, the truth is when it comes to retirement planning there is no one size fits all plan of attack that works for everyone in every situation.

I think the real question we all have to ask is how adverse is the retiree to losing money/risk. Most retired people have a lower risk tolerance, especially if they have six figures stashed away in a bank account collecting dust.

If you were on the flipside of the coin and shopping for an annuity. How would you find it suitable? Here is what the 2010 NAIC model regulation says to consider,

"...the insurer or insurance producer shall have reasonable grounds for believing that the recommendation to purchase an annuity or exchange an annuity is suitable for the consumer based on the facts disclosed by the consumer as to his or her investments and other insurance products and financial situation and needs, including the consumer's suitability information."

Also, the NAIC model requires us to have a reasonable basis for believing the consumer would benefit from certain features of the annuity and that any underlying subaccounts are suitable for the client.

For an indexed strategy or immediate income strategy the following are usually important 'needs' of a retired person:
- Not running out of money.
- Principal Protection
- Preservation of Capital
- Having Something to Leave Behind

- Complimenting Social Security
- Hedging Against Loss

But Mike, is health of the annuitant a concern?

Yes, it's the primary concern depending on the strategy you choose to implement. Remember, an annuity contract does have life insurance components and health should always be a factor to consider and that the client carefully considers before purchasing an annuity.

"If everyone is thinking alike, then somebody isn't thinking." **– George Patton**

Chapter 5: Marketing Annuities?

Annuities are not usually bought they are sold. So, where do we look for buyers? Let's break down the demographics.

The 2013 Survey of Owners of Individual Annuity Contracts found some interesting statistics to start our search for buyers. The research found that the Age at which First Annuity was purchased was as follows:
- Under 50 years old 39%.
- 50 to 64 years old 47%.
- 65 years and older 14%.

The study also found that the majority of individual annuity owners were in fact female, but only slightly.

Furthermore, the study found that among annuity owners.
- 58% were Married
- 24% were Widowed

- 10% were Single Never Married
- 7% were Divorced.

The study found that among owners their employment status was as follows:
- 65% Retired.
- 20% Employed Full Time
- 8% Employed Part Time.
- 3% Homemaker.
- 4% Other.

The last point I want to pick out of that study was that it found Household Income to be as such:
- 5% Under $20,000
- 16% $20,000 to $39,999
- 14% $40,000 to 49,999
- 25% $50,000 to $74,999
- 20% $75,000 to $99,999
- 13% 100,000 to $199,999
- 7% $200,0000

This shows that the average premium on an annuity is around $60,000 and 60% of annuity owners make less than $74,999 combined adjusted gross income. Which would basically equate to a family both working part time or close to full time.

But Mike, How can we use this information?

Success leaves clues. So, that being said, we are looking for pre-retirees between the ages of 50 to 65, who are married or single and a majority of these people are making less than $75,000 in household income.

Think of a few places where you might find those people in large groups. Also, remember we are looking for people with in excess of $50,000 in savings and with a target premium of over $100,000 in savings.

The first thing that probably comes to my mind is a mobile home park. Not the most likely of spots, but it fits the parameter of what the study found and most likely they do not work with a financial planner. Help the underserved and it will usually reap rewards.

Remember, with insurance it's important to focus on base hits and not just homeruns. If you have the market for those households that earn $200,000+ then go for it. But, if you can pick up a $60,000 annuity each month, then go for it.

For me as a rule of thumb, I always go where others are not. I go into a space and try to dominate that space. Before you start running around to mobile homes pitching annuities make sure you check with Department of insurance regulations and your TPA for adequacy.

Another great opportunity for annuities would be pre-retiree government bodies. If you can get large groups of police officers, teachers, and or medical professionals.

Meeting with the Decision Maker.

Are you meeting with the decision maker? It's best to be straight forward and ask. Because, wouldn't you want to know if the person you are speaking with is the one who signs the application?

It will save you a tremendous amount of time in your qualifying process to flush this out. Don't not talk to someone because they can't make a decision but include the person who makes the decision in the conversation. If someone needs approval from a spouse, great let's meet all together to discuss this.

Find a Mentor

I started right out of college selling insurance and consulting insurance professionals. There is no way I would have learned as much as I have without having a good mentor. I've had several and let me tell you successful people will tell you how they became successful.

Some people don't really know how to illustrate processes but you can learn tips and tricks. It's paramount you find someone who knows what they are talking about. If you want to be the best you have to seek out the best and learn.

"If you want truly to understand something, try to change it." – **Kurt Lewin**

Chapter 6: Areas of Concerns for Retirees

In insurance we all see people deal with the same three problems during retirement. Someone gets sick and racks up medical bills not covered by insurance and pass on extreme debt. Someone runs out of money because of a bad investment strategy or because they become severely ill.

During the distribution phase of retirement the primary concern shifts from growth to sustainability and preservation of capital. So, how do we deliver that preservation of capital and that peace of mind?

3 Concerns/Challenges that face every Retired Person

1. You live too long and run out of money.
2. You live too long and get sick or terminally ill.

3. You live too short and run out of savings in a Nursing Facility.

We've addressed some of the monetary concerns earlier in this book. But, the main concerns are overarching concerns in everyone's retirement plan. For instance, what happens if a client works with a financial planner and decides that they need income until age 90. Because, the average life span is 80 years old in America and life expectancy in his family is around average. But, with life extending technology what happens if he lives to 100? No one wants to be the guy who runs out of money.

What happens if you live long but towards the end of your years you become terminally ill and rack up extreme medical debt due to being forced into a nursing home?

What happens if you get seriously injured or sick and rack up bills but then die under the average life expectancy.

These are all situations we never want to think about but insurance is a cost effective way to handle these concerns. Long-term Care built into life insurance is the easiest solution, some annuities even have riders that can help in certain situations.

"When a person's interested in something, they're willing to tolerate any kind of problems that may come up." **– Cus D'Amato**

Chapter 7: 3 Primary Sources of Retirement Income

We're going to breakdown the three main sources of retirement income that most prospects rely on for retirement.

1. Social Security (Fixed Amount)
2. Qualified Plan / Company Pension
3. Personal Savings

Understand Social Security and potential pitfalls.

Social Security is projected to run deficits by 2032. Which means that we will have more people taking from the system than people putting money into the system for the first time in history. So, what does that mean? It means one of three things happen:

- The government reduces benefits.
- The government increases taxes.

- The government does nothing until the system goes bankrupt.

The Social Security system was created for a limited number of people and expanded over the years. When the system was created the average life span was around 55 years old and is now around 80 years old. When the system was create there were 5 workers paying for a single retiree and now the ratio is about 2:1.

Why Annuities compliment Social Security in a retirement plan.

62% of beneficiaries received AT LEAST HALF of their income from social security.

Qualified Plan or Pension Plan

According to a recent study done in the Washington Post, "Only **7 percent** of employers studied offer new employees traditional pensions, which pay out a certain amount at retirement based on a worker's pay and how long they stayed with a company."

Today most Qualified Retirement Plans are usually offered are 401(k) plans. 401(K) plans have limitations as far contribution and distribution of funds. But, overall they are good retirement vehicles. The one big consideration here is how much tax liability does this create and how long can someone live off of their 401k earnings? Unless you have a crystal ball that might be hard to determine.

Why do people have money in their savings account?

Well Mike, because one day I imagine they want to spend it. Or to perhaps have a rainy day fund of some kind. Either they are going to liquidate the money and use it for retirement or they are fearful of some looming unexpected expense. So, I present a follow question to you.

What emergency expenses would you need to use your savings for?

The most obvious expense would be for a nursing home or the cost of in-home nursing care. Which is probably the most burdensome and large expense facing our seniors today. Other expense considerations:
- Aging Home
- Insurance Deductibles
- Burial Expenses
- New Car or Transportation Costs

"Knowledge comes, but wisdom lingers. It may not be difficult to store up in the mind a vast quantity of facts within a comparatively short time, but the ability to form judgments requires the severe discipline of hard work and the tempering heat of experience and maturity."
Calvin Coolidge

Chapter 8: How Annuities can fill the gap for a retiree.

Qualifying Process

1. What part of your retirement is guaranteed?
2. Would you be interested in learning about guaranteed products?
3. What do you like about your current retirement plan?
4. What kind of changes do you want to see in your retirement plan?
5. What is more important to you peace of mind or earnings?
6. Are you the decision maker in your family in regards to financial advising or choosing financial products?
7. What does this client want? What does this client need?
    a. I want to leave money to my family after I pass.

      i. Why is that important to you?
8. Are you happy with the current rate of savings on your savings account or CD?
9. Would you mind if we...
10.   How does it sound so far...
11.   If I could find a product that has zero risk and guarantees a stream of income for life, would you be open to looking at it?

Selling Yourself.

How do you build trust? How do you help a customer know, like and trust you? How do you show a customer you care? Start by asking questions but then when you set expectations let them know why you do what you do. What is your reason? What is your story? We all have this yearning to follow people worth following, give them a reason to follow you.

Analyze Current Retirement Plan

When you analyze a retirement plan remember although there is a new fiduciary rule in place, you are not technically a fiduciary. Because, you cannot make financial decisions for a client without client consent. A fiduciary is someone who can do that.

What I'm trying to convey is that you should not start trying to reallocate invested funds or money going into investment products. Look for low handing fruit. Look for money sitting in savings accounts. And for E&O purposes make sure you get everything in writing, especially if the client wants to reallocate funds.

Explain/address the Areas of Concern.

This part of the conversation is the, 'what happens if' part of the conversation.

1. You live too long and run out of money.

2. You live too long and get sick or terminally ill.
3. You live too short and run out of savings in a Nursing Facility.

Fill the Gaps / Design a Plan

As an Agent if you plan on using these two strategies. Ask yourself, does the client have life insurance in place and long term care?

If the client has LTC and life insurance go with the indexed/variable approach. If they are more risk adverse go with the variable annuity approach.

But Mike, what if the client does not have Life Insurance and or does not have long term care insurance?

Tax Advantages of this strategy?

Long Term Care can be tax deductible up to a certain amount of the premiums depending on the plan. So, check with your CPA and the Client's CPA before executing this strategy with a client.

Major Downsides of this plan.

1. Long term care has an elimination period from 30 to 90 days.
2. Annuities have surrender periods.
3. Life insurance has surrender periods.

But Mike, if we are selling peace of mind how do we justify the drawbacks?

There is a price for liquidity and there is a price for guarantees. There is a price for everything. Remember this is the most stable aspect of a retirement plan. There is not potential for loss and the insurance companies pay into a reinsurance fund protecting up to 250,000 of your money. Much in the same way that the FDIC insures a bank account.

Client Example

Let's say you have a healthy couple of health individual with $240,000 in savings earning less than 1% interest. They have their home paid off and low or no credit card debt. You've spent the time to analyse their financial needs and determine that they have no life insurance, they have no long term care insurance and there is a definite need for an annuity.

Let's say after speaking with the client age 60 to 65 we uncover these needs and discover an interest to purchase an annuity. But, we also need to protect against illness or high medical bills due to long term care.

What we can do is take a lump sum of $150,000 to $160,000 in an immediate life-only annuity. So, why would we do this? The customer would have enough saved for emergencies in savings, but would earn more than the interest was paying out on the savings account.

The main reason we would do this is to fund a Long Term Care policy and a GUL. Or find a way to build LTC into the permanent life insurance. There are pros and cons to either option. LTC can be tax deductible up to certain amounts given certain circumstances, but in a life policy is cheaper to purchase. It's cheaper in a life policy because it usually just expiates a death benefit that would have been paid anyways. In a life policy there is no elimination period for LTC. Weigh the pros and cons with each client and go from there.

Let's say we go with the Standalone LTC product. We would purchase a policy with a lifetime benefit of around $170,000 to $180,000 or a monthly benefit of around $5000 to $6000. The premium would be somewhere in the ballpark of $350 per month.

Now how do we pay for the Long Term Care? Simple, the immediate income from the annuity provides a monthly payout factor of around $700 for the life of the annuitant. Now since we are investing a large sum of the client's capital in an annuity and the annuity payments run the length of the annuitants life we need to hedge our bets. We then place a $150,000 to $160,000 permanent life policy on the client in case they die prematurely. This would be somewhere in the ball park of $200 per month depending on health and product selection.

The net financial result to the client would be 3 products that would cost about $600 per month and leave about $200 per month in excess income. Obviously, these are estimates. The net result to the client's retirement plan is that it protects against premature death. It protects against living too long and fear of running out of money. It protects against a client getting sick and entering a nursing home facility.

What we are doing here is leveraging assets to provide peace of mind and help seniors deal with unforeseen costs during retirement.

Address Possible Objections

- I heard annuities are bad investments.

- - Why? Just dig. Usually this springs from a CPA or some kind of television personality who has a vested interested in managed funds… But, again don't try to take positions and tell someone they are wrong. Just try to understand and pivot.
- Can't you just give me a quote over the phone?
  - I sure could and I am sure there are lot of Agent who would do just that. This is a real policy and my job is to make sure that I know who I am insuring. But, aside from that it's also my job to make sure we explain the insurance/investment in a way that is easy to understand and answer any questions you might have. (address concerns)
- If I need the money I can't access it.

- Liquidity has a price. Much like how accessing money in a 401K before a certain age results in an extra tax penalty.
- If I die tomorrow the life insurance company keeps everything? This is why we purchase the life insurance with part of the income provided by the annuity.

Building a Fact Finding Sheet

I've seen some great fact finding sheets and some that need improvement. Here are some of the questions and topics you should always address in a fact finding sheet.

1. Having a commitment on the fact finding sheet prior to the proposal stage. Not a financial commitment but a commitment of will to go through the presentation. "I John Snow, request the projected amount of money needed during my retirement, assuming I want to reitre at age 65..."
2. Current Life Insurance

3. Current Liquid Assets
4. Current Non-liquid Assets
5. Current Income
6. Spouses Current Income
7. Beneficiary
8. Employer Name
9. Vacation Time if still working.
10. Projected Retirement
11. Pensions?
12. Smoker?

Pro's and Con's of Annuities

Pros

Lifetime Income – with an immediate annuity we are getting the client a guaranteed periodic payment as long as they live. The insurance company is taking a risk some people die soon and some live long.

Inflation Protection – Annuities have inflation riders much like other life insurance products to keep pace with inflation. There is a high degree of customization in the annuity market.

Principal Protection – If we go with the Indexed Annuity then the principal is protected against any loss, because we cap the gain and the insurance company keeps the difference.

Cons

Lower Returns on Your Investment – The trade off for an annuity is capital growth potential. We are limited by growth and shrinkage. Protection comes at a cost.

High Costs: Some annuities offer a 10% commission and high management fees which can eat away at gains or lower the ceiling for some products.

Inflexible – Annuities like all retirement vehicles are meant for long term growth potential and thus are inflexible to some extent.

Summation

Thanks for reading my book. Please leave me a review on Amazon or read one of my many other books on selling insurance. Each is different and provides unique insights... I hope. Thanks again!

www.ingramcontent.com/pod-product-compliance
Lightning Source LLC
Chambersburg PA
CBHW030505220526
45464CB00006B/2666